The Little Yogi
By S.G. Bloomfield

Illustrated by: Kate Chirko

THE LITTLE YOGI

Copyright © 2023 by S.G. Bloomfield

All rights reserved. No part of this publication may be reproduced, distributed, or transmitted in any form or by any means, including photocopying, recording, or other electronic or mechanical methods, without the prior written permission of the publisher, except in the case of brief quotations embodied in critical reviews and certain other non-commercial uses permitted by copyright law.

First Edition: 2023

Design and layout by Stefania Grieco

Published by Stefania Grieco

Hardcover ISBN: 978-1-7390129-1-5

Paperback ISBN: 978-1-7390129-0-8

E-book ISBN: 978-1-7390129-2-2

To all the little yogis of the world,

This book is dedicated to you, the shining stars of mindfulness and growing wisdom. May it guide your breath and uplift your spirit.

Your dedication to yoga strengthens your body and mind, fostering love, kindness, and compassion for all. As you explore inner landscapes, you shape your life and the world.

Remember that yoga's gift is not only in the poses but in the friendships, laughter, and joy you experience. You represent unity and a hopeful future.

Cheers to you, tiny warriors of peace, as you grow strong, vibrant, and luminous, carrying ancient wisdom into the world.

Namaste, young yogis, and may yoga's magic be with you always!

With love and light,

S.G. Bloomfield

Once upon a time, there was a young child named Max.

Max had a tough day at school and was feeling very sad and upset.

Max's mom saw how upset Max was and decided to share a special book called "The Little Yogi."

Max and his mom began to read the story of the Little Yogi,

who discovered the power of yoga and mindfulness to bring peace and happiness to his life.

Inspired by the Little Yogi, Max decided to try some yoga poses.

His mom joined in, and they both smiled, enjoying the shared experience.

As they continued practicing,

Max and his mom tried the Warrior Pose, feeling strong and confident.

They also practiced the calming Child's Pose,

The next day at school, Max faced a difficult situation with a classmate.

Using kind words and understanding, Max resolved the conflict with his classmate,

who was surprised and grateful for Max's patience and empathy.

spreading joy and laughter as they practiced various poses together.

Max was excited to share his newfound yoga knowledge with his friends during recess.

Max also introduced his friends to mindfulness and meditation,

helping them find a moment of peace and focus amidst the excitement of the playground.

After school, Max returned home and eagerly shared his day with his mom.

Max and his mom talked about how yoga and mindfulness had made a positive impact on Max's life at school.

He felt a sense of warmth and understanding, grateful for the Little Yogi's lessons.

Max continued to practice yoga and mindfulness, standing tall and confident in his room.

And so, Max and his friends continued to practice yoga and mindfulness, discovering the power of the Little Yogi's teachings.

Together, they found happiness, peace, and unity, sharing the magic of the Little Yogi with everyone around them.

The End

Bonus Activities: Discover the Magic of the Little Yogi

Breathing Colors

Instructions: Sit comfortably with your back straight. Close your eyes and take deep breaths. As you breathe in, imagine the air filling your body with a calming color. As you breathe out, imagine any negative feelings leaving your body with each exhale. Practice this exercise for a few minutes, and use the space below to write or draw how it made you feel.

Gratitude Tree

Instructions: On the leaves of the tree below, write or draw things you are grateful for. Take a moment to think about each one as you add it to the tree. When you feel sad or upset, look at your Gratitude Tree to remind yourself of the positive things in your life.

Yoga Adventure Storytime

Instructions: Create your own yoga adventure by making up a story that includes the yoga poses you've learned from the Little Yogi. Use the space below to write or draw your story. Share your story with your friends or family, and have them act out the poses as you tell the tale.

_____
(YOUR TITLE HERE)

_____
_____
_____
_____
_____
_____
_____
_____
_____
_____

Mindfulness Coloring Page

Instructions: Find a quiet and comfortable spot. As you color in the picture of Max and their friends practicing yoga, take deep breaths and focus on the present moment. Notice the colors and textures of the coloring page, and enjoy the process of creating a beautiful scene

The Little Yogi Word Search Puzzle

Instructions: Find the words listed above in the puzzle. Circle or highlight each word as you find it. Enjoy and have fun!

D	Y	G	Q	O	N	A	S	J	R	H	S
R	O	P	E	A	C	E	F	U	L	Y	S
I	G	G	U	G	J	C	U	T	E	R	E
M	A	X	Z	R	O	B	E	L	E	E	N
D	H	A	P	P	Y	w	W	C	S	O	L
L	M	E	D	I	T	A	T	I	O	N	U
S	S	E	R	G	O	R	P	L	P	Z	F
F	U	N	F	U	L	R	S	A	E	L	D
S	S	E	N	D	N	I	K	U	E	O	N
H	U	G	S	G	T	O	S	G	R	V	I
C	A	R	E	B	Q	R	E	H	T	E	M
P	L	A	Y	G	R	O	U	N	D	Y	R

WORDS LIST:
1. MAX
2. YOGA
3. WARRIOR
4. MEDITATION
5. TREEPOSE
6. MINDFULNESS
7. PROGRESS
8. PEACEFUL
9. PLAYGROUND
10. KINDNESS

CAN YOU FIND 4 MORE WORDS?

Hints:

Look carefully, some words might be spelled backwards!

Words might be hidden diagonally, not just up and down or side to side.

Longer words are often easier to spot than shorter ones.

If you can't find a word, try looking at the puzzle from different angles

About the Author page

About the Author: S.G. Bloomfield is a self-taught artist and registered yoga instructor who is passionate about sharing the benefits of yoga and mindfulness with people of all ages. Born and raised in Canada, S.G. Bloomfield currently resides in Belize, Central America. After completing their yoga teacher training on November 11, 2017, they were fortunate enough to teach Kid yoga and Puppy yoga at the same yoga studio where they trained. In addition to the Little Yogi series, S.G. Bloomfield has also written a guide for adults, helping them embrace their inner light through the practice of yoga. They are the owner, designer, artist, and photographer behind Home Time Art, an Etsy shop offering modern, minimalist, nursery, spiritual, and yoga high-quality printable art as instant downloads. S.G. Bloomfield is dedicated to providing unique, personalized designs that bring joy and beauty to people's lives.

About the Illustrator page

Kate Chirko is a Ukrainian artist and illustrator whose true passion lies in creating enchanting illustrations for children. With a focus on children's books, Kate's delightful and whimsical paintings are loved by both young readers and adults alike. Fluent in conversational English, she effortlessly brings stories to life through her incredible attention to detail and innate artistic talent. Using tools like Photoshop and Procreate, Kate's skills are truly impressive. Clients from around the world are drawn to her work and often return for more, captivated by her ability to capture the essence of a story. Kate Chirko is hailed as an amazing artist, leaving customers thoroughly delighted with their experience. Connect with her on Facebook and Dribbble using her handle, @katechirko, to witness her remarkable illustrations that will transport you to a world of imagination and wonder.

More Adventures Await!

Get ready for more exciting stories with Max and their friends as they continue to explore the world of yoga, mindfulness, and friendship in our upcoming Little Yogi series. Here's a sneak peek at what's to come:

"**Max and the Magical Yoga Forest**"
Join Max on a magical journey to a yoga forest inhabited by wise animals and mesmerizing landscapes. Max learns new yoga poses, practices mindfulness, and befriends enchanting creatures in this captivating adventure.

"**Max and the Mindful Moon**"
Max brings the joy of yoga and mindfulness to their community by hosting a unique Mindful Moon Festival. Alongside friends, they create an enchanting night of yoga, meditation, and activities that unite everyone under the moonlit sky.

Stay tuned for these exciting new stories and more. We can't wait to share them with you!

Thank You for Reading!

We hope you and your little ones have enjoyed the adventures of Max and their friends in our Little Yogi series. Your feedback is incredibly valuable to us, and we would be grateful if you could take a moment to share your thoughts by leaving a review.

Your review will not only help us improve our future books but also allow other parents and children to discover the magic of yoga, mindfulness, and friendship in these heartwarming stories.

To leave a review, please visit the website or platform where you purchased the book.

Thank you once again for your support, and we can't wait to continue sharing the Little Yogi's journey with you!

Warmly,

S.G. Bloomfield

Author of the Little Yogi series

www.ingramcontent.com/pod-product-compliance
Lightning Source LLC
Chambersburg PA
CBHW042248100526
44587CB00002B/59